EXPLORE
GRAVITY!

Cindy Blobaum

Illustrated by Bryan Stone

Newest titles in the **Explore Your World!** Series

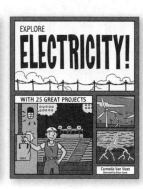

Nomad Press
A division of Nomad Communications
10 9 8 7 6 5 4 3 2 1

This book was manufactured by McNaughton & Gunn, Inc., Saline, MI USA.
November 2013, Job #497064
ISBN: 978-1-61930-207-5

Illustrations by Bryan Stone
Educational Consultant, Marla Conn

Questions regarding the ordering of this book should be addressed to
Nomad Press
2456 Christian St.
White River Junction, VT 05001
www.nomadpress.net

**Nomad Press is committed to preserving ancient
forests and natural resources.**

We elected to print *Explore Gravity! With 25 Great Projects*
on paper containing 100% post consumer waste.

CONTENTS

TIMELINE

Circa 340 BCE: In Greece, Aristotle describes a model of gravity pulling everything to round layers surrounding the earth.

Circa 150 CE: In Egypt, the mathematician and astronomer Claudius Ptolemy publishes the *Almagest*, a set of 13 books showing the math behind the movements of the sun, moon, and planets. This book was used as the main astronomy textbook for over 1,300 years.

1487: The astronomer Nicolaus Copernicus creates a model of the solar system showing the earth and the other planets orbiting the sun in circular paths. Earlier models showed the earth at the center of the solar system.

1400s

1700s

1800s

1798: Henry Cavendish measures the force of gravity between two masses.

1845: John Couch Adams and Urbain Le Verrier use Newton's laws of gravity and observations of the planets to predict the existence of a planet past Uranus. The next year, Neptune is discovered.

IV

TIMELINE

1589: Galileo Galilei proposes that all objects fall at the same rate, no matter their size.

1609: Johannes Kepler combines math, Copernicus's model of the solar system, and observations of the planets and stars to create three new laws about the elliptical orbits of planets.

1678: Robert Hooke invents the spring scale and introduces Hooke's Law about how much force it takes to stretch a spring a certain distance.

1687: Sir Isaac Newton publishes his Universal Laws of Gravity.

1900s

1916: Albert Einstein publishes his Geometric Theory of Gravitation.

1942: Germany's V2 rocket overcomes the earth's gravity and reaches outer space.

1957: The Soviet Union places the first satellite, named *Sputnik*, into space.

1969: American astronaut Neil Armstrong becomes the first human on the moon.

1986: The Soviet Union begins construction of Mir, the first space station to continuously orbit the earth.

1998: Construction of the International Space Station begins.

2000s

2004: NASA launches the Gravity Probe B to measure differences in gravity around the earth.

2012: NASA maps the gravity of the moon using GRAIL Probes.

INTRODUCTION

Wherever you are right now, point a finger straight **down**. Change your position and point straight down. Stand up. Stand on your head. Lie down. Did you point to the same spot? How do you know which way is down?

These questions may seem simple, or even silly. Of course you know which way is down. Down means toward the ground. When you are standing, down means toward your feet. If you stand on your head, down means below your head. If you are sitting in a desk chair, down goes by your side.

WORDS to **KNOW**

down: toward the ground. If you're underground, down means toward the center of the earth.

On the earth, the **force** of **gravity** pulls everything toward its center. There are forces pushing and pulling **objects** all the time. Wind pushes tree branches and sailboats. Your muscles push and pull parts of your body so you can walk, talk, and move.

You can see some forces, but you can't see gravity. It's **invisible**. You can choose to use many forces, but gravity is different. You can't turn it on or off. It pulls you down whether you want it to or not. Without it, you would float away!

How does gravity keep you safe? Why does the position of your belly button matter? How do **astronauts** work in zero gravity? Can gravity make life easier? You'll learn the answers to these questions and more in this book!

WORDS to KNOW

force: a push or a pull.

gravity: a natural force that pulls objects to the earth.

object: something that can be seen or touched.

invisible: unable to be seen.

astronaut: a person who travels or works in space, where the moon, sun, planets, and stars are.

matter: something real that takes up space.

scientist: someone who studies science and asks questions about the natural world, seeking answers based on facts.

WHAT'S THE MATTER?

Gravity works on all **matter**. Matter is the word **scientists** use to describe anything that takes up space. You can measure matter, even though sometimes you can't see it or touch it. Water is matter, and so is air and gases.

INTRODUCTION

Chocolate cake is matter. It takes up space. You can stick a fork in it, and describe how it looks and tastes. A feather is matter, and so are dogs and cats, a car, this book, your body, and even a speck of dust.

Gravity's force is a natural **attraction** that affects all matter. Gravity pulls all matter closer together. There is gravity between an apple and a banana sitting on a table. There is gravity between a bird and a tree. Most of the time, the pull of gravity between objects is so small that we don't notice it. But the more matter an object has, the stronger its pull.

WORDS to KNOW

attraction: an invisible power that pulls things together.

gravitational pull: the force of gravity acting on an object.

The earth is very, very big. Its **gravitational pull** is stronger than anything else around it. Earth's gravity pulls you, the air, plants, trees, and even the moon, closer to its center. It keeps our feet on the ground!

What isn't matter? Your thoughts and feelings. They are real, but they don't take up space. You can't touch or measure them. Gravity isn't matter. It doesn't take up space and you can't touch it.

Did You Know?

The sun's gravity is pulling at you, but it's so far away you don't notice it. Earth is by far the biggest, closest object to humans, so it has the strongest pull on us.

3

Make a Science Journal

A science journal is a great place to note the steps of your experiments, make **observations**, and record **data**. A scientific method worksheet is a useful tool for keeping your ideas and observations organized. The scientific method is the way scientists ask questions, form a **hypothesis**, and then find answers.

SUPPLIES

↗ plain paper

↗ stapler

↗ markers

↗ pencil

1 Stack about five sheets of paper and fold them in half.

2 Staple along the folded edge about 1 inch in (2½ centimeters) to secure the pages together.

3 Decorate the cover any way you want. Just don't forget the word *Gravity* and your name.

4 Use the inside pages to make scientific method worksheets for the experiments you'll do in this book.

WORDS to KNOW

observation: something you discover using your senses.

data: a collection of facts.

hypothesis: a prediction or unproven idea that tries to explain certain facts or observations.

SCIENTIFIC METHOD WORKSHEET

QUESTIONS: What is the point of this activity? What am I trying to find out? What problem am I trying to solve?

EQUIPMENT: What did I use?

METHOD: What did I do?

HYPOTHESIS/PREDICTIONS: What do I think will happen?

RESULTS: What actually happened? Why?

ACTIVITY

Find Straight Down

Gravity pulls everything down toward the center of the earth. How can you prove which way is straight down? Where is straight down when you are standing on a hill?

Why do you need to know which way is straight down? If you drop something, you want to know where to look for it. Builders want to make sure their buildings are straight and don't lean sideways. Trees need to be planted vertically or they might fall over.

Caution: Ask permission to do this experiment. Be careful not to drop anything on another person, your pet, or anything that might break.

1 Stand, holding an object, such as a shoe, in the palm of your hand. Turn your hand over and let it go. A line from your hand to where the object first lands is a **vertical** line, one that goes straight up and down.

2 Do the same thing with the book, pencil, and ball. Down is the direction each item falls. Is down different for the different items? Of course, the ball might roll a bit after it hits the ground!

THINGS TO TRY: What happens if you drop the objects from a tree or a second-story window? What happens if you toss them up first?

SUPPLIES

➔ several different objects to drop, such as a shoe, book, pencil, and ball

➔ several different places to drop the objects from

WORDS to KNOW

vertical: straight up and down.

JUST for FUN

Mom: Why are you still in bed?
Kid: Gravity is pulling me down!

5

Growing Down

Plant roots grow down and stems grow up. Roots bring plants the water they need. Stems hold leaves up toward the sun so they can make food.

Do roots grow down because water is stored in the soil or because gravity pulls them down? Start a scientific method worksheet in your science journal to track your steps.

1 Soak the beans overnight in a cup of water.

2 Fold each paper towel in half, then fold it again. Put one in each bag. It should fill the bottom half of the bag.

3 Pour about 2 tablespoons of water into each bag. You want the paper towels to be damp, but not dripping wet.

4 Staple each bag in three evenly spaced places about 2 inches from the top of the bag (5 centimeters). This makes four spots for seeds.

SUPPLIES

- ↗ science journal and pencil
- ↗ 16 dried lima beans (other dry beans work too)
- ↗ cup
- ↗ water
- ↗ 4 paper towels
- ↗ 4 zippered sandwich bags
- ↗ tablespoon
- ↗ stapler
- ↗ sunny window with sill or flat surface
- ↗ tape

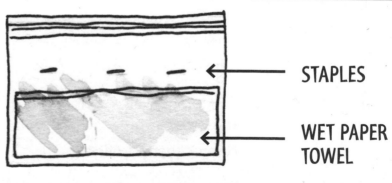

STAPLES

WET PAPER TOWEL

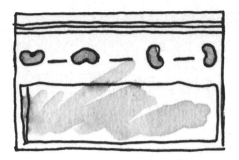

5 In one bag, place a bean in each space between the staples. Change the direction of the bean each time. Start with the first bean facing up, then down, then right, then left. Repeat this in the same order for each bag.

6 Zip the bags shut. Find a window that gets a lot of sunlight.

- Tape one bag to the window with the zipper on top.

- Tape one bag to the window with the zipper at the bottom.

- Tape one bag to the window with the zipper facing right or left.

- Lay one bag flat on the window sill or a flat surface with the same sunlight.

7 Check on your seeds every day. In what direction are the roots growing? Is gravity at work? Record your observations. It is possible that some beans might not **sprout**.

WORDS to KNOW

sprout: to start growing.

THINGS TO TRY: What happens if you change the direction of the bag after the roots have started to grow?

Finding Down with a Plumb Bob

In ancient times, as early as the pyramids in Egypt, builders used a tool called a plumb bob, which uses gravity to find a vertical line. A simple plumb bob is a small, heavy object on the end of a string. Plumb bobs always point straight down.

1 Tie one end of each string to the center of a pencil. Tie one item to the other end of each string.

2 Hold the pencil at each end and lift up. What happens to the object at the end of the string? What happens if you tilt the pencil so one end is higher? Repeat this with each pencil and item.

THINGS TO TRY: What happens when you try to use each plumb bob near a refrigerator? In a tub of water? In front of a blowing fan? Which item makes the best plumb bob? How might this be a helpful tool for you?

SUPPLIES

- ➚ 4 pieces of string, each 3 feet long (1 meter)
- ➚ 4 pencils
- ➚ 4 different items of different weight (craft stick, magnet, small plastic toy, nail)

Did You Know?

In some old churches, skyscrapers, or buildings with domes, you can still see how plumb bobs were used to keep buildings straight. Look for a metal plate in the middle of the lowest floor of the building. Builders hung a bob over that plate. As the building got taller, they moved the string higher, keeping it straight over the plate.

GETTING TO KNOW GRAVITY

Before you were born, you floated around in fluid inside your mother. You didn't feel gravity's pull because the fluid held you up. This means your muscles didn't have to work very hard.

As soon as you were born, your body felt the full pull of gravity. Your muscles were so weak you couldn't even lift your head. Your parents had to hold it up for you. They also had to pick you up and move you around. As you grew, you practiced pushing against gravity. Your muscles grew stronger. You learned to lift your head. You did your first push-ups. Then you learned to crawl, walk, and even jump.

KNOWING UP AND DOWN

While your muscles were getting stronger, your brain was learning to use the information your body was sending it. When you are standing, gravity is pulling all your matter toward the bottom of your feet. Your brain learned to recognize this feel of gravity's pull as down.

Your body sends the same signals when you are lying down and standing on your head. Your brain uses these signals to tell you which way is down. Scientists call this **body sense**.

You also use your ears to know which way is down. If you could look inside an ear past the **eardrum**, you would see three tiny tubes bent almost like horseshoes.

Did You Know?

The daily pull of gravity is strong enough to make you shorter! Measure your height as soon as you get up one morning. Spend the day running, jumping, and playing, then measure your height again right before you get into bed. Are the numbers the same, or did you shrink? Most people are a little bit shorter at night, after gravity has been pulling them down all day.

WORDS to KNOW

body sense: when your body sends signals to your brain to help it tell which way is up and which way is down.

eardrum: the part of the ear that separates the inside of the ear from the outside.

WORDS to KNOW

calcium: a mineral found mainly in the hard part of bones.

nerve: a bundle of thread-like structures that sends messages between different parts of the body and the brain.

sense of balance: when your eyes, ears, and body sense all work together to help you stay upright and not fall over.

level: straight across, not tilted.

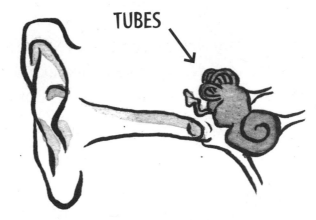

TUBES

There is hair, fluid, and tiny bony crystals made of **calcium** in these tubes. If your head is upright, the fluid and crystals are around the hairs at the bottom of each tube. When you move your head, gravity pulls the fluid and crystals in one or more of the tubes to the new, lower place. As the crystals move, they also move different hairs. All the hairs are connected to **nerves**. The nerves send a message to your brain telling you which way is down. This is known as your **sense of balance**.

ARE YOU LEVEL?

After 25 to 30 seconds of tilting your head, the fluid and crystals in your ears settle in place. Then tilted feels **level**. This is okay if you are lying in bed, but it might mean trouble for a pilot flying a plane in the clouds. Pilots need to know when a plane is turning or moving up or down. If a pilot was making a long, tilted turn but her ears told her she was flying level, she could get confused. That's one reason planes have instruments and computers to help pilots.

Your brain also uses your eyes to help you know up and down. You see the sky over your head. Your brain has learned that the sky is up. The ground is down. But your eyes are easy to trick.

That's why a print made by graphic artist M.C. Escher is so confusing. It shows people walking up walls and upside-down on stairs. Doors and trees are sideways. It's hard to tell which side of the picture is up and which is down!

It doesn't really matter whether you know down and up when you are just looking at a picture. But you might get confused when it's really dark. You'd probably move slowly. You might tilt your head or hold your arms out in front of you. You are using your body sense and sense of balance.

TRY IT: TEST YOUR GRAVITY SENSE

If you want to give your sense of gravity a real test, go to a fun house that has rooms with slanted floors. This confuses your sense of balance. To trick your eyes, there might be fake windows with pictures of the sky at the bottom and the ground at the top. There might be tables bolted to the ceiling. These tricks can confuse your brain so much that you find it hard to walk! What's the best way to get it straight? Trust your body sense. Let gravity pull you down to your hands and knees, then crawl through the fun house.

Did You Know?

Knowing about gravity can help people get out of danger if they are buried in snow from an **avalanche**. The snow that surrounds their bodies lifts them up so it doesn't feel like gravity is pulling them down. Their heads can be tilted for so long they don't know which way is up. Their senses might not be working right, but gravity is! If they cry or spit, gravity will pull the water down. Then all they need to do is dig the other way—up—and out of the snow!

MEASURING GRAVITY

Scientists like to measure things. One way to measure how gravitational pull feels on your body is called the **G-force** or Gs. Here on the earth, you usually feel a G-force of 1. Higher Gs feel like gravity is pulling you down extra hard. Your body seems heavier and it takes more energy to move.

WORDS to KNOW

avalanche: a large amount of snow that slides down a mountain very quickly.

G-force: a measure of the force of gravity.

Imagine that first you lift something that weighs 10 pounds at a G-force of 1. At a G-force of 2, it would feel like you were trying to lift something that weighed 20 pounds.

13

G-forces also measure how fast something changes speed. When you jump off a step or even sit down quickly, the G-force you feel goes up a little. You also feel higher Gs when you go up in an elevator or airplane, speed up in a car, or zoom off on a roller coaster ride. Gravity hasn't changed, so why does it feel like it's pulling you harder? Your body is used to feeling a G-force of 1. When you suddenly speed up, all your skin, blood, muscles, and bones are pulled a little harder than you're used to. This makes it feel like the base gravitational pull affecting you has increased.

Sometimes you feel less Gs. Try jumping up in an elevator that is going down. For just a second, you will feel lighter. When you are headed downhill on a roller coaster, you are falling at the same **rate** as your seat. But you don't feel gravity pulling on you. You feel like you would fly away if the seat belt wasn't holding you in. The feeling that there is no gravity pulling you down is called zero-G.

WORDS to KNOW

rate: the speed of something measured in an amount of time, such as miles per hour or feet per second.

JUST for FUN

How many Gs are in the biggest roller coaster in the world?
Two—in the word *biggest*!

G-WHIZZ!

There's a special plane called Zero-G. People, including astronauts, use it to feel what it's like to be almost weightless. First, the pilot flies the plane up at a steep angle. During this time, everyone feels about 1.8 Gs. Then the pilot zooms down at a steep angle. Suddenly, everyone feels almost 0 Gs for 10–20 seconds. The pilot flies up and down like this 12–15 times! Most people who ride in Zero-G get sick from so many changes in the G-force. That's how this plane got its nickname, the Vomit Comet!

People go very fast in a lot of sports, like running, jumping, skiing, skateboarding, or riding bobsleds and luges. Everyone doing these things feels changes in Gs for a short time. Ski jumpers and skateboarders might feel lighter than air when they leave the ground. Lugers, lying on their backs as they zip downhill on small sleds, feel much higher Gs. Pilots, astronauts, and racecar drivers can also feel wide ranges of G-force.

Most people can't handle anything higher than 5 Gs for longer than a few seconds. The muscles in your heart and lungs aren't strong enough to pump blood to your brain under those conditions. Astronauts, fighter pilots, and racecar drivers go through special training and sometimes wear special suits so they can handle up to 9 Gs for short periods of time.

COMMON G-FORCES

WHERE	G-FORCE	HOW LONG?
Carnival spinner (Gravitron, Silly Silo)	up to 3	about 1 minute
Space Shuttle	1.7–3	8.5 minutes
Extreme Roller Coasters	3.5–6.3	2–5 seconds
Luge (sled)	5.2	less than 1 minute
Formula One Race Car	5–6	1–3 seconds in a turn
Apollo 16 spaceship	up to 7.19	10–15 minutes
Fighter pilots	up to 9	10–20 seconds

Personal Anti-Gravity Machine

You have your very own **anti-gravity** machine—your muscles! The muscles going from your lower back to your feet do most of the pushing against gravity. If you don't like gravity making you shorter, you need to make these muscles stronger. Get ready to give your anti-gravity machine a workout!

WORDS to KNOW

anti-gravity: free from the force of gravity.

SQUATS: (10–25, each day)

1 Stand with your feet under your shoulders and your arms out in front.

2 Keeping your back straight, bend your knees like you're sitting. Stop when your thighs are level with the ground. Keep your back straight and stand.

TOE RAISES: (30–50, three days a week)

1 Stand with your feet apart and slowly push your heels off the floor until you are balanced on your toes.

2 Slowly lower your body down until your heels are on the floor.

BOTTOM BUSTERS: (5, five days a week)

1 Lay on your belly and bend your knees so your heels face up.

2 Squeeze the muscles in your rear end as you lift your knees off the floor. Your heels should push toward the ceiling. When you can't lift any higher, hold for two seconds. Relax your muscles as you slowly lower your knees to the floor.

On the Straight and Level!

In the introduction you made a plumb bob that used gravity to make sure things are vertical. Now you can make a water level, a tool that uses gravity to make sure things are straight across! The water level works because when water is in a confined space, gravity makes sure the top of it is level.

Caution: This activity is best done outside.

1 Fill both cups about half full with water. Stand them side by side. Notice how the water goes straight across. Tilt one cup slightly, but not enough to spill it. Look at the water—is the top of it tilted or straight across? Compare the top edges of water in both cups.

2 Add several drops of food coloring to the water and stir to mix.

3 Use one or more clothespins to clamp one end of the clear plastic tubing closed. Place this end into a bucket on the ground.

4 Insert the funnel into the open end of the tubing. Slowly pour the colored water into the tube. Do not fill it all the way. There should be a few inches of empty space at the end.

SUPPLIES

- ↗ 2 clear cups
- ↗ water
- ↗ food coloring
- ↗ spoon
- ↗ 10–15 feet of clear plastic tubing
- ↗ clothespins or other clamps
- ↗ bucket
- ↗ funnel
- ↗ 8–10 books

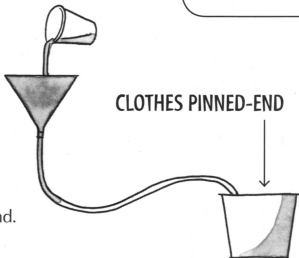

CLOTHES PINNED-END

5 Hold both ends of the tube up at the same height. Remove the clothespins from the clamped end. The water line should move until it is at the same level on both sides. If it isn't, that means there are air bubbles in the tube. Gently tap the sides to get the air bubbles to move out.

6 Go to a flat place. Make two stacks of books about 10 feet apart. One person should hold one end of the open tube so the water level is lined up with the top edge of one pile of books. Another person should hold the other open end of the tube near the top edge of the second pile of books. It is okay if some of the tube is just lying on the ground. You know the stacks are even if the water lines up exactly with the top of both stacks. If they are not even, add or remove books to each stack until they are even.

7 Use the level to see if a table, deck, or fence top is level.

THINGS TO TRY: What happens if you put the stacks of books on stairs or a small hill? Use the level to find things that are at the same height in other parts of the room or yard.

Did You Know?

Airplanes have an instrument in the cockpit that works like a level. It is called an attitude indicator. It can tell pilots if their wings are level and if the nose of the plane is pointing up toward the sky or down toward the earth.

19

GRAVITY BASICS: MATTER AND MASS

When scientists talk about gravity, they use the words matter and **mass**. Matter is everything that is real that you can measure. One way that scientists compare matter is to talk about its mass. Mass is the amount of matter in an object. The more matter there is in something, the more mass it has. What if you blow up a balloon until it's the same size as your head? The balloon is full of air and your head is full of your brain. Both the balloon and your head are matter. They are real and you can measure them. But which one has more mass? Your head does, of course. It has more matter in it than the balloon has.

If an object doesn't change, then its mass doesn't change. You can throw the balloon into the air, drop it in a pool of water, or take it to the store. It will still have the same mass. Of course, if you let air out of the balloon, you have changed it. Then there would be less matter in it. So it would have less mass.

Scientists use a **balance** to compare the mass of different things. A balance is a tool that can be as simple as a long bar with a hook on each end. To make a balance work, you try to get the same amount of mass on each end. When you do this, you can hold the balance in the middle and it will stay level. If one side has more mass than the other, that side will go down. You can use a balance to compare the masses of very different things. For example, how many marshmallows do you think are needed to equal the mass of a marshmallow-sized rock?

WORDS to KNOW

balance: a tool that shows if the mass of objects is even.

Did You Know?

This type of balance would show you the same results on the moon, Mars, or even Jupiter!

TRY IT: FEEL THAT MASS

Instead of comparing marshmallows and rocks, scientists use the kilogram as their measure of mass. A kilogram is the mass of 1 liter of water. If you have a liter bottle in your house, fill it with water. Lift it to see what 1 kilogram of mass feels like. Scientists have calculated that the mass of the earth is 5,972,200,000,000,000,000,000,000 kilograms. That's a lot of mass!

Balance can be a tricky word. The tool called a balance is used to compare the mass of two things. When you use a balance, you try to make its two sides level.

Another way to use the word balance is to think about keeping things from falling over. If you try to stand on one foot, you might lose your balance and fall over. Why? Because you have more mass on one side than the other. The side with more mass is pulled down.

WORDS to KNOW

center of balance: the point on an object where its mass is even all the way around.

center of gravity: the point on an object where it can be supported and stay in balance.

To keep matter from falling over, you need to find its **center of balance**. This is also called the **center of gravity**. All matter has a center of gravity. Earth has a center of gravity. So do you. So do rocks, hammers, pencils, and shoes.

IS EARTH'S "CENTER" CENTERED?

The center of gravity for the earth is not in its center! You might think of the earth as being a big ball, but it really isn't. There are tall mountains and deep valleys. If you took all the water away, it would look bumpy and lopsided. Since the earth is not even, there are some places with more mass and some places with less. This means the pull of gravity is a bit stronger in some places and a bit weaker in others.

 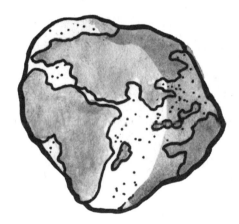

Sri Lanka, an island off the tip of India, has the lowest pull of gravity on the planet. Scientists think it might be because of the way melted lava, or magma, is moving under the crust. If you visit there, you might be able to jump a bit higher than usual. You might not feel like jumping at all if you climb to the top of a mountain in the Himalayas, like Mount Everest. Although gravity is stronger than average there, it would be all the climbing gear you were carrying that would pull you down!

If the mass in the matter is spread evenly, then the center of balance is in the middle. This means you could balance the object on that center point and it would stay level. The center of balance of this book is near the middle.

CENTER OF BALANCE

If the mass of an object is uneven, then the center of balance will not be in the middle. A hammer has a lot more mass at one end than the other. If you wanted to hold it at one spot and have it balance and stay level, you need to hold it very close to the end with more mass. That spot would be its center of gravity, even though it is not in the middle.

Did You Know?

The names of some common measurements come from the things people have used to balance masses of different objects. In the past, precious gems like diamonds were balanced against carob seeds. Today the mass of diamonds is measured in something called a carat. Meat and wool were measured against stones. Some people in Great Britain still use a stone (14 pounds) as a unit of measure for body weight. And bullets were once balanced against grains of barley. Today the mass of a bullet is listed in grains.

TRY IT: CENTER CHALLENGE!

Put one finger under each end of a ruler. Move both fingers toward each other at the same time. When your fingers are together, the ruler is balanced. That is the center of gravity. Measure the distance to each end. Do the same thing with a broom. Do you get the same results?

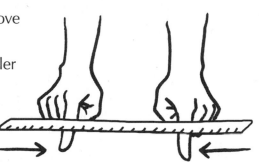

Some matter that has more mass at one end is described as having a high center of gravity. This means more of the mass is on the upper part. Things with a high center of gravity fall over more easily. This is good if you are a gymnast, diver, or high jumper. A high center of gravity makes it easier to jump or do flips.

Some things have a low center of gravity. This means more of their mass is on the lower part. Things with a low center of gravity are more **stable**. Football players and race cars perform better with a low center of gravity. It is harder to push them over. Brooms have a low center of gravity. Can you balance a broom on the bristle end? What about on the handle end?

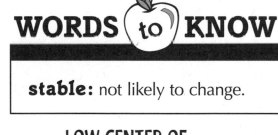

WORDS to KNOW

stable: not likely to change.

LOW CENTER OF GRAVITY

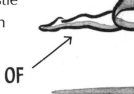

HIGH CENTER OF GRAVITY

Fingertip Balance

You can compare the mass of small objects using this paper balance.

1 Use the hole punch to make three holes in each cup. You want them evenly spaced just under the top rim.

2 Cut three 12-inch pieces of string for each cup (30½ centimeters). Thread one end of a piece of string through each hole and tie it so that the cup hangs from the three strings.

3 Gather the loose ends of the strings from one cup together. Tie these ends together. These cups will be useful in several activities in this book.

4 Copy this pattern on the cardboard and cut it out.

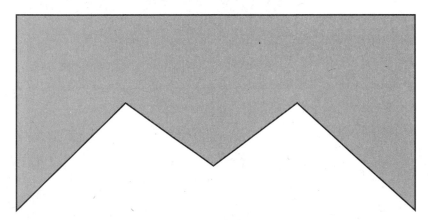

5 Try to balance the middle tip of the card on the tip of one finger.

6 Put a paper clip on the bottom tip of each side. Try to balance it again.

SUPPLIES

↗ hole punch
↗ 2 small paper cups
↗ scissors
↗ string
↗ ruler
↗ pencil
↗ thin cardboard (an index card or cereal box)
↗ scissors
↗ 2 paper clips
↗ pennies
↗ nickels

7 Hang a cup from each paper clip. Put a penny in one cup and a nickel in the other. Is the balance level?

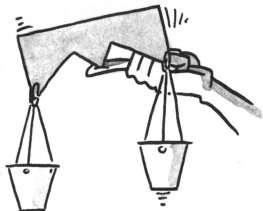

8 Add more pennies or nickels to each side until they are balanced. How hard is it to make the two sides balance?

THINGS TO TRY: You can use your balance to compare the masses of other small objects. You can also make balances of different sizes. Does the size of the balance make any difference in how it works? What happens if you make a balance that is not even on both sides?

BELLY BUTTON SCIENCE

Scientists have studied athletes to discover if they can **predict** who will be the faster runners and swimmers. One thing they compared was the height of athletes and the height of their belly buttons. Your belly button is your center of gravity. They discovered that if you have two athletes of the same height, the one with the higher belly button will be the faster runner. This athlete has a higher center of gravity. The one with the lower belly button will be the faster swimmer. This athlete has a lower center of gravity.

WORDS to KNOW

predict: to say what will happen before it really happens.

Balance + Sculpture = Mobile

In 1931, artist Alexander Calder invented a new form of art. He hung a small wooden ball at one end of a rod. At the other end of the rod, he hung a heavy cast iron ball. He attached a wire at the center of balance and hung the rod from the ceiling. When the heavy ball was tapped, it made the lighter ball spin around. Calder had made the first **mobile**—art that used gravity to work! You can use your knowledge of gravity and balance to make your own piece of gravity art for your room.

1 Use the end of a paper clip to poke a hole near the end of one of the straws. Thread the paper clip through the hole so it hangs down from the straw. Repeat this so you have a paper clip hanging down from both ends of all 3 straws.

WORDS to KNOW

mobile: a construction or sculpture made of balanced wire and shapes that can be set in motion by the movement of air.

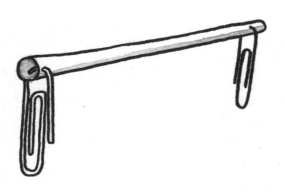

2 Use the end of a paper clip to poke a hole all the way through the center of each straw. Thread the paper clips through so they point up from the straw.

3 Make six chains by hooking paper clips together. They should be different lengths.

4 Thread one chain through the paper clip at the end of each straw.

5 Take one of the straws with its two paper clip chains. Attach these chains to the middle paper clips of the other two straws.

6 Now have some fun coloring and cutting out four paper letters, shapes, or pictures. Do you want your mobile to have a theme, such as a trip to the beach or all the musical instruments played by members of your family? Thread your papers through each open end of your paper clip chains. Make one more paper clip chain. Thread it through the middle of the top straw of your mobile. Hold the mobile by this paper clip chain. Is your mobile balanced? If not, what can you do to make it balanced?

7 Hang your mobile from the ceiling where it can move freely and dance in the wind!

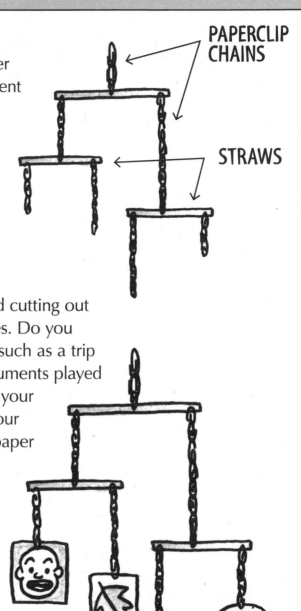

PAPERCLIP CHAINS

STRAWS

Where's Your Center of Gravity?

When you are standing, your center of gravity is over your feet. Your mass is spread around equally. This is true for everyone. To see if you have a high or low center of gravity, you are going to have to get off your feet.

1 Kneel on the floor. Set the box down in front of you.

2 Bend forward until your arms are flat on the ground. Your elbows should be bent so they are touching your knees. Put your hands together with your fingers pointing away from you. Move the box so it is at the tips of your fingers.

3 Kneel back up. Put your hands behind your back. Lean forward and try to knock the box over with your nose without falling or putting your hands down.

SUPPLIES

↗ small box, such as a matchbox or individual-size cereal box, or rectangular block

WHAT'S HAPPENING? If you fall over, you have a high center of gravity. If you don't fall over, you have a low center of gravity. Can you change your center of gravity? What if you add mass to the lower part of your body?

THINGS TO TRY: Ask your friends and people in your family to try this experiment. Start a scientific method worksheet and keep track of the age and gender of each person who tries. You can make a chart to organize your data. Do you notice any patterns?

DISCOVERING GRAVITY

Even before anyone ever heard of gravity, it was clear something was pulling things down. A rock thrown into the air falls to the ground. Water runs down a hill, not up. Is it harder to lift a log than to let it fall? Everyone knows the answer!

Aristotle was a famous Greek **philosopher** around 330 **BCE**. He explained gravity by saying that all matter had a place it was supposed to be. This was called its natural place. The natural place for most things was to be near the center of the **universe**.

WORDS to KNOW

philosopher: a person who thinks about and questions the way things are in the world and in the universe.

BCE: put after a date, BCE stands for Before the Common Era and counts down to zero. CE stands for Common Era and counts up from zero. The year this book was published is 2013 CE.

universe: everything that exists everywhere.

Aristotle imagined the whole universe to be like huge see-through balls wrapped around each other. He thought that the natural place for the earth was in the very center, with layers for each planet, the moon, and the sun. He believed everything moved to its natural place based on whether it was heavy or light.

An object with mass would fall toward the center of the earth and the heavier it was, the faster it would fall. Lighter things like gases would drift upward, toward the layers of the moon and the planets.

Many of Aristotle's ideas tried to explain the way things are in the world and in the universe. But did everyone agree with everything Aristotle thought? Philosophers and scientists are always asking questions and disagreeing with each other.

In 1543, a scientist from Poland named Copernicus wrote that the earth was not the center of the universe. He thought the sun was at the center. Then around 1589, an Italian scientist named Galileo argued that a heavy ball and a light ball fall at the same rate. If this was true, scientists needed a new idea to explain why things fell toward the earth.

Aristotle's view that the universe was made of layers of balls was not something he could test. People just had to believe him. But could people test whether light and heavy things fell at different rates? When Galileo started thinking that a heavy ball and a light ball would fall at the same rate, people tested his idea. How? By dropping two objects with different masses at the same time and watching what happened.

THE FORCE OF AIR

Have you ever seen a leaf, feather, or snowflake float slowly to the ground? If Galileo's idea was correct, shouldn't they fall fast, like everything else? They would if the air pushing them up wasn't there! Air **resistance** can push against gravity. For really heavy things, air doesn't make much of a difference. But for light, flat things, like leaves and feathers, the force of air pushing up can really slow things down! To really see everything fall at the same rate, the falling test needs to be done in a **vacuum**. A vacuum is a place where there is no matter, not even air. Scientists have made special vacuum tubes to run experiments. And in these vacuums, a flat, light feather falls at the same rate as a round, heavy rock.

WORDS to KNOW

resistance: a force slowing down another force.

vacuum: a space with nothing in it, not even air!

After many tests, people agreed that objects fall at the same speed. If you drop a hammer and a marshmallow at the same time, they land at the same time. Next, scientists wanted to measure just how fast these objects were falling.

When you drop an object, it is said to be in **free fall**. This is when an object is falling without anything to speed it up or slow it down. A stick dropped off a bridge would free fall. A parachute on the stick would make it go slower, so it would not be in free fall. A jet engine on the stick would make it go faster. That would not be free fall either.

WORDS to KNOW

free fall: to be pulled through the air by only the force of gravity.

FREE FALL

NOT FREE FALL

JUST for FUN

Which of the armed services is the strongest?
The Air Force!

Scientists timed how long it took for the same object to fall from different heights. They saw that as things fall, they speed up. Eventually, scientists figured out that an object in free fall on the earth falls 32.2 feet per second per second (9.8 meters per second per second).

What does that mean? It means that in the first second an object is falling, it travels 32.2 feet (9.8 meters). As it falls, it speeds up. In the second second, it goes 32.2 + 32.2 = 64.4 feet (9.8 + 9.8 = 19.6 meters). In the third second, it speeds up even more and travels 32.2 + 32.2 + 32.2 = 98.6 feet (9.8 + 9.8 + 9.8 = 29.4 meters)!

After a while though, a falling object stops speeding up. It can't go any faster. It keeps going at the same speed. That speed is called its **terminal velocity**.

English scientist Isaac Newton read about what others were doing. He agreed with the ideas of Copernicus that the moon, sun, and stars were not stuck in see-through layers as Aristotle described. But he still wanted to know, "Why do things fall toward the earth?"

He thought about this question for many years. He wrote letters to other scientists. He told them he wondered why apples falling from trees hit the ground. Why didn't they fly up? Why didn't they go sideways? He knew some people believed things fell because the earth attracted them. And why did heavy and light things fall at the same rate?

WORDS to KNOW

terminal velocity: the fastest an object will travel in free fall.

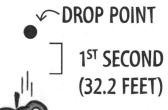

DROP POINT

● 1ST SECOND (32.2 FEET)

2ND SECOND (64.4 FEET)

$$32.2$$
$$+\ 32.2$$
$$64.4$$

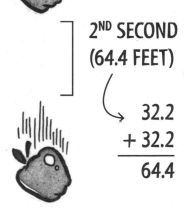

3RD SECOND (98.6 FEET)

$$32.2$$
$$32.2$$
$$+\ 32.2$$
$$98.6$$

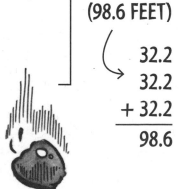

Newton thought about things in the sky, too. Why did the moon stay in a circle around the earth? The moon never fell onto the earth, but why didn't it float away? Was the earth falling in a circle around the sun? Everything on the earth and in the sky seemed to be falling toward something else. Was it the same force?

WORDS to KNOW

orbit: the path of an object circling another object.

scientific law: a description of something that happens in nature, but not why. Scientific laws are based on observations.

In 1687, Newton wrote about a force that makes all objects attracted to each other. He invented a new math called calculus to explain how this force worked all over the universe. It works to keep us on the ground and it works to keep the earth **orbiting** the sun. From the Latin word *gravitas*, which means heaviness, he wrote, "It is now established that this force is gravity, and therefore we shall call it gravity from now on."

Newton did not know why there was gravity. He used what he saw to explain gravity. To do this he came up with some basic rules about gravity. Other scientists read Newton's book. They used his math to predict what would happen if anything fell, anywhere, and they agreed with him. His work became known as Newton's **scientific law** of universal gravity.

Here are Newton's basic rules for gravity.

✳ Gravity is a force of attraction.

✳ There is gravity between all objects.

✳ Gravity pulls things toward the center of each object.

✳ The more mass an object has, the stronger the pull of its gravity.

✳ The closer two things are together, the stronger the pull of gravity.

Many scientists used Newton's laws to make new discoveries. They wanted to measure, for example, how hard gravity was pulling things down. They knew a marshmallow landed with a soft plop and a hammer with a hard thud. How could they measure how hard gravity was pulling on these different masses?

JUST for FUN

Gravity is a law. Lawbreakers will be brought down!

Did You Know?

As scientists in more recent years have made and used better tools, they have discovered that some facts Newton used to develop his laws of gravity were wrong! Even though Newton did have some errors in his work, his law of gravity is still good enough to explain how we expect most things in the universe to work. But keep your eyes open. Can you find his mistakes?

WORDS to KNOW

weight: a measure of the gravitational pull on an object.

Between 1658 and 1678, English scientist Robert Hooke had done some tests with a spring. He knew a spring could be pushed together or pulled apart. He found that how far a spring was pulled out or pushed together depended on the amount of force used on it. When gravity is the force pulling down on a spring, you can measure how far the spring moves. So by using a spring, scientists could measure the pull of gravity on one object at a time. They called this new measurement **weight**.

A bathroom scale with a dial works this way. The dial on the scale is connected to a spring. When something is put on the scale, it presses down the spring. The more the spring is pressed down, the higher the number you see on the dial. The higher the number, the more something weighs. The greater the weight, the stronger the force of gravity pulling on the object.

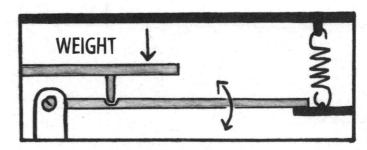

WEIGHT

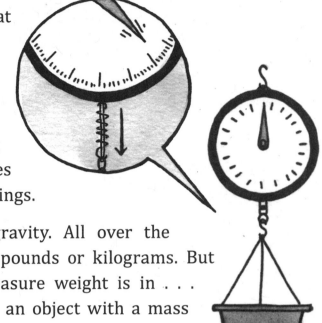

A scale at the grocery store that weighs fruits and vegetables also works this way. Have you ever done this? You put your food in a tray hanging off a spring that's attached to a dial. As the spring stretches, the hand on the dial moves up. This is another way to weigh things.

Weight is a force caused by gravity. All over the world, people measure weight in pounds or kilograms. But guess what? The real way to measure weight is in . . . Newtons! Anywhere on the earth, an object with a mass of 1 kilogram (2.2 pounds) weighs close to 10 Newtons (really it's 9.8). If you could take that object to the moon where there is less gravity, it will weigh less.

TRY IT:
SPRING ACTION

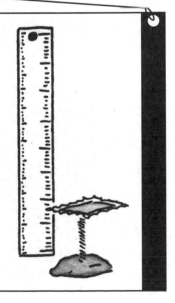

Take a spring out of a pen. Stand the spring upright on a piece of tape or small bit of clay. Stand a ruler behind it. Record the height of the spring. Put a stamp on top of the spring. Record its height. Put a paper clip on top of the spring. Record the height. Which item is gravity pulling on more?

Measuring Air

Isaac Newton said that gravity exists between all things that have mass. Does air really have mass? Is it really pulled down by gravity? Make a balance and see!

SUPPLIES

↗ string
↗ scissors
↗ 2 balloons
↗ stiff ruler

1 Cut two pieces of string about 6 inches long (15 centimeters).

2 Tie one end of one string to an empty balloon. Tie the other end to the 1-inch mark on the ruler (2½ centimeters).

3 Blow air into the other balloon and tie the end shut. Tie one end of the other string to the balloon with air. Tie the other end to the 11-inch mark on the ruler (28 centimeters).

4 Put a finger under the 6-inch mark on the ruler (15 centimeters) and lift up. Which end of your balance is heavier?

JUST for FUN

What's as big as you but doesn't weigh a thing?
Your shadow.

THINGS TO TRY: Can you think of a way to make the ruler balance?

See the Pull of Gravity

Aristotle believed heavy things fell faster than lighter ones. Galileo believed all things fell at the same rate. Which one do you believe? Start a scientific method worksheet to organize an experiment to investigate this idea. When you drop several different items, which one do you think will fall the fastest? Which one will fall the slowest?

1 Hold the shoe in one hand, the pencil in the other.

2 Raise your hands until they are both shoulder high. Drop both items at the same time. Does one fall faster? Does one hit the ground before the other? Make a chart to record your observations in the scientific method worksheet.

3 Take turns dropping any two of your objects at the same time. Does one fall faster? Record your observations.

4 What can you conclude from your data? Does your conclusion support your prediction?

THINGS TO TRY: What happens when you drop the same pairs of items from a second-story window?

SUPPLIES

- ⇗ science journal and pencil
- ⇗ several items to drop, such as a paper clip, shoe, rock, marble, pencil, coin, and ball
- ⇗ a friend to help you observe

41

ACTIVITY

Free Fall vs Foot Fall Race

Can you run 322 feet (99 meters) as fast as a ball can fall? Try it and see! The key to setting up the race is to remember a falling object goes faster each second. So the distance you need to run each second will get bigger!

SUPPLIES

↗ tape measure
↗ large open space
↗ 4 craft sticks
↗ stopwatch

1 Measure a distance of 322 feet (99 meters).

2 Label the craft sticks: **1st second** 32.2 feet (9.8 meters) per second, **2nd second** 64.4 feet (19.6 meters) per second, **3rd second** 96.6 feet (29.4 meters) per second, and **4th second** 128.8 feet (39.2 meters) per second.

> 1st Second , 32.2 Ft. per second
> 2nd Second, 64.4 Ft. per second
> 3rd Second, 96.6 Ft. per second
> 4th Second, 128.8 Ft. per second

3 Place a craft stick at each of these distances: **32.2 feet (9.8 meters)**, or the distance an object free falls in the first second; **96.6 feet (29.4 meters)**, or the total distance an object free falls in two seconds (32.2 + 64.4); **193.2 feet (58.8 meters)**, or the total distance an object free falls in three seconds (32.2 + 64.4 + 96.6); and **322 feet (99.0 meters)**, or the total distance an object would free fall in four seconds (32.2 + 64.4 + 96.6 + 128.8).

32.2 feet	96.6 feet	193.2 feet	322 feet
1ST SECOND	**2ND SECOND**	**3RD SECOND**	**4TH SECOND**
32.2 feet/second	64.4 feet/second	96.6 feet/second	128.8 feet/second

4 Try the race two ways. Time how long it takes you to run 322 feet (99 meters). Then measure how far you can run in four seconds.

THINGS TO TRY: What happens if you set up the racecourse going downhill? Or run on a windy day with the wind at your back? Do you think you are running your fastest, at terminal velocity, between the first two sticks or the last two sticks? How can you find out?

TESTING FREE FALL

People today are still testing ideas about free fall and terminal velocity. In October 2012, Felix Baumgartner rode a **helium** balloon up and up, high above the earth. He had to wear a special suit to protect him from the cold. He also had to carry **oxygen** because the **atmosphere** miles above the earth does not contain enough oxygen to breathe. When he was 24-miles high (39 kilometers), he jumped out, but he did not open his parachute for over 4 minutes. As Baumgartner was in free fall, he reached a speed of 834 miles per hour (1,342 kilometers per hour). This is the highest terminal velocity ever experienced by a human.

WORDS to KNOW

helium: a light gas often used to fill balloons.

oxygen: a gas in the air that people and animals need to breathe to stay alive.

atmosphere: the blanket of air surrounding the earth.

Elevator Experiments

An elevator is a great place to test some ideas about gravity. Try to pick a time when no one else needs it.

1 Copy the chart on the next page into your science journal so you can record your experiment results.

2 Stand on the bathroom scale. Write down the number. This is your weight and a measure of how much gravity is pulling you down.

3 Watch the dial as you bend your knees, stand on tiptoes, and then jump. Did you notice the number change? Did the number go up or down?

SUPPLIES

↗ science journal and pencil

↗ portable bathroom scale with a dial

↗ 8 pennies

↗ 2 cups with strings from Chapter 2

↗ fingertip balance from Chapter 2

↗ 2 paper clips

↗ elevator

4 Put four pennies in each cup. Use a paper clip to attach one cup to each side of the balance. Put the balance on the tip of one finger. Watch as you bend your knees, stand on tiptoes, and then jump. Does either side of the balance change?

5 Take the scale and balance with you into the tallest, fastest elevator you can find. Start at the lowest level of the building. Stand on the scale and record the number. Press the button for the highest floor. Watch what happens to the number on the dial as you rise. Does the number go up or down? Repeat the test going down. Does the scale act the same way?

6 Start at the lowest level again. Put the balance and cups on a finger. Press the button for the highest floor. Watch the balance as you rise. Does either side rise or fall? Repeat the test going down.

WHAT'S HAPPENING? The spring scale measures weight, which is the pull of gravity. Your weight will change in the elevator as the G-force changes. It will go up when you feel more G-force. It will go down when you feel less G-force. The balance is comparing mass. It will stay in balance as long as there is a G-force of any strength.

INSTANCE	NOTES
Scale when bending knees, standing on tiptoes, and jumping	Did the numbers on the scale change?
Finger balance when bending knees, standing on tiptoes, and jumping	Did the finger balance change position?
Scale in the elevator	What happened to the scale numbers when you went up? What happened when you went down?
Finger balance in the elevator	What happened to the finger balance when you went up? What happened when you went down?

GRAVITY IN SPACE

Isaac Newton's scientific law of gravity explained that the earth's gravity pulls on the moon and the moon's gravity pulls on the earth. These ideas may have begun with the work and ideas of ancient scientists.

WORDS to KNOW

tide: the daily rise and fall of the ocean's water level near a shore.

new moon: when the moon is directly between the earth and the sun so it is not clearly visible or seen as just a tiny sliver.

Scientists keep records of what they see around them. Then they can look at the records to see if there are any patterns. One pattern noticed a long time ago is that the ocean's **tides** are higher when there is a full moon or a **new moon**. Why does this happen?

Isaac Newton believed his ideas on gravity explained how the tides and the moon are connected. He wrote that because the earth and moon both have mass and are so close to each other, the gravity of each pulls on the other. You can see the pull of the moon's gravity on the water of the oceans. The moon's gravity causes the tides.

JUST for FUN

What's an astronaut's favorite drink?
Gravi-tea!

But why are tides higher during a full moon and new moon? At these times, the sun, moon, and earth are lined up in a row in space. The pull of gravity from the moon and sun work together to move the water more than at other times.

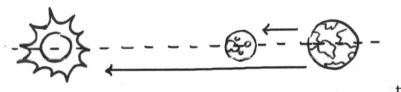

Since the earth is bigger than the moon, its gravity pulls harder on the moon than the moon pulls on the earth. It pulls on the moon so hard that the moon cannot move any farther away from the earth.

Imagine you attach a magic pen to a baseball. The pen draws a line in the air that marks where the ball goes. If you hit the ball, the force of gravity pulls the ball closer to the earth a little at a time. So the line is a curve. The bigger your hit, the larger the curve.

Newton thought of the moon and the earth as giant balls. He knew that balls are curved and that they fall in a curve when they are hit or thrown.

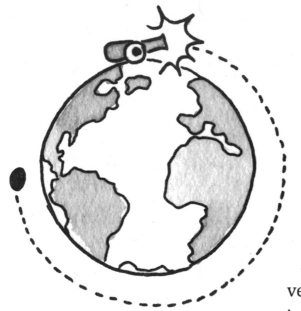

WORDS to KNOW

theory: an idea that tries to explain why something is the way it is.

centripetal force: the inward force that keeps an object moving at a steady speed in a circular path around another object.

To explain his **theory**, Newton drew a picture of a mountain and a cannonball. If you could shoot a cannonball high enough and fast enough from the top of a very tall mountain, it would fall in a circle all the way around the earth. Why would the curve of its fall match the curve of the earth? Because gravity pulls with the same amount of force everywhere on the earth.

The matching curves of the falling ball and the earth would mean that gravity would keep pulling the ball down in the same curved line. It would never land. Newton named this **centripetal force**. He wrote that gravity, working as centripetal force, is what keeps moons moving around planets and planets moving around the sun.

THE MOON

People have studied the moon for a long time. They've asked, "How big is the moon? How far away is it? Why does it travel in a circle around the earth? Is the moon bare because everything floated away?"

WORDS to KNOW

estimate: a best guess using facts you know.

To **estimate** the size of the moon, people measured things on the earth. They compared these measurements to the moon in the sky. They used math to estimate the size of the moon and the distance between the earth and the moon.

Isaac Newton made his own estimates of the moon's size and its distance from the earth to explain his law of gravity. He also estimated the mass of the moon. Newton used these numbers to estimate the pull of gravity on the moon. How could anyone check Newton's ideas? Go to the moon!

TRY IT: ESTIMATION STATION

Test your estimation skills! Fill a big jar and a small jar with the same type of small items, like marbles, pasta, or beads. Empty the small jar and count the items. Use that number to estimate how many are in the big jar. Write down your estimate. Empty the big jar and count. Don't feel bad if your estimates are not close. Newton's estimate of the mass of the moon was wrong!

WORDS to KNOW

NASA: National Aeronautics and Space Administration, the U.S. organization in charge of space exploration.

It took many years and a lot of work before scientists were ready to test Newton's ideas in space. On July 20, 1969, **NASA**'s Lunar Module *Eagle* landed on the moon. Was Newton's scientific law right? Would the gravity on the moon be less than the gravity on the earth? With the cameras rolling, astronaut Neil Armstrong stepped down a ladder wearing a 180-pound space suit (82 kilograms). Even with all that extra weight, he had no trouble walking!

On a later trip, astronaut David Scott tested Galileo's findings that objects fall at the same speed. The moon was a perfect place for a test because objects are almost in a vacuum. There is no air resistance. When he dropped a feather and a hammer at the same time, they landed at the same time. Galileo's law was right!

MODERN MOON MAP

In 2012, two **space probes** the size of washing machines followed each other in orbit around the moon for several months. They stayed close to the moon's surface. When the front probe passed over something with more mass, gravity pulled it a bit harder. It speeded up and the distance between the two probes increased. Special instruments on each probe measured that distance. Scientists used those numbers to figure out the mass of the area below the probes. They made a map showing how the mass changed around the moon.

WORDS to KNOW

space probe: a spacecraft used to explore the solar system and transmit data back to the earth.

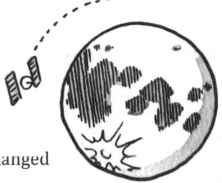

Did You Know?

Because there is no atmosphere on the moon, there is also no wind or weather. Footprints from astronauts who walked on the moon over 40 years ago are still there and it will probably take another 10 to 100 million years before they are covered by dust.

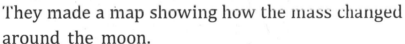 MOON —— 238,900 MILES —— EARTH

THE SPACE SHUTTLES

Scientists all over the world are interested in doing experiments in a place with low gravity. They want to know how plants, animals, crystals, and science tools act in space.

WORDS to KNOW

microgravity: when something acts like there is no gravity because it is in free fall or in orbit around the earth.

International Space Station (ISS): a science lab in orbit about 200 miles above the earth.

In 1981, NASA launched its first space shuttle, which is like a giant glider. A rocket provided the energy to lift it 200 miles above the earth (322 kilometers). Once it was past the earth's atmosphere, the shuttle glided around the world in a circle. It fell at 17,500 miles per hour (28,000 kilometers per hour). This speed kept the shuttle falling around the curve of the earth, just like Newton described. Earth's gravity was still pulling on the shuttle. But everything on the shuttle was in constant free fall. People floated like there was no gravity pulling them down. Scientists call this **microgravity**.

THE INTERNATIONAL SPACE STATION

The shuttles were good, but they could only be used for 17 days at a time. Scientists wanted to study how things worked in microgravity over long periods of time. Several countries worked together to create the **International Space Station (ISS)**.

The ISS is a permanent research lab that orbits 200 miles above the earth (322 kilometers). Scientists around the world send experiments to the station. Astronauts live on the station for months at a time doing experiments. When new astronauts come to the ISS, the other astronauts travel back to Earth. Sometimes they bring the results of their experiments with them.

Did You Know?

The gravity on the moon is too weak to even hold air around it! Gravity is what holds the earth's atmosphere around the earth. Without gravity we wouldn't have the air we breathe.

	PULL OF GRAVITY	LONGEST STAY BY ONE PERSON	SAMPLE EXPERIMENTS
Moon	one-sixth of Earth's	Over 3 days (75 hours)	Collect rocks, feather and hammer drop, hit golf balls.
Space Shuttle	Microgravity (weightless)	17 days	Toys in space, the smell of a rose, growing crystals.
International Space Station	Microgravity (weightless)	215 days (over 7 months)	How to clean air, what happens to monarch caterpillars, growing plants.

Scientists are studying microgravity and weightlessness for many reasons. One reason is that someday humans might travel to the planet Mars. A trip to Mars would take between 150 and 300 days. It would take just as long to get back to Earth. So Mars astronauts would be in space for almost two years!

On a trip that long, astronauts would need to be able to grow food. Experiments on the ISS test which plants grow and the best way to take care of them. Astronauts are also testing how to keep their muscles strong and their bodies healthy. Bodies change in space. Muscles don't have to push against gravity so they get weaker. Even hearts are affected. Scientists want to find ways to keep people healthy in space. The tests they do might also help keep people healthy back on Earth.

BLACK HOLE

Space scientists like to study stars, too. Stars are the most massive things in space. Stars are heavy balls of energy. Sooner or later, the energy burns out. All the atoms that created that energy are still there. When stars burn out, there is no energy, heat, or light moving out. The only force at work is gravity. The pull of gravity is very, very strong. Everything nearby is pulled toward that space. Scientists call that area a **black hole**. The nearest black hole is 1,600 **light years** away from Earth.

WORDS to KNOW

black hole: a place in space where gravity is so strong even light gets pulled in.

light year: the distance light travels in one year.

OTHER SPACE EXPLORATION

NASA has already sent some unmanned spacecraft to Mars and other planets. They have sent telescopes and probes into deep space. To get there, gravity gives the spacecraft bursts of power on their trip. They aim the spacecraft so it will go close to a moon or another planet. As the spacecraft gets close to the object, it starts to get pulled in by that object's gravity. That speeds up the spacecraft. With the right timing and a boost of power, the spacecraft then shoots out of the orbit with a burst of extra speed, just like a rock leaving a slingshot. This is called **centrifugal force**.

WORDS to KNOW

centrifugal force: the outward force on an object moving in a curved path around another object.

LIFTOFF

Did You Know?

Most birds do not have the same throat muscles you do. To get a drink, they dip their beaks into water, get a mouthful, then tip their heads back to swallow. Without gravity, they can't drink! So birds like robins, blue jays, and sparrows can never live on a space station where there is no gravity. But pigeons and hummingbirds can!

TRY IT: SPEED BOOSTER

Find a park that has a pole or skinny tree in the middle of a field. Run toward the pole as fast as you can. When you get close, reach out one arm. Grab the pole, swing halfway around and let go. Keep running in the new direction. Do you feel the extra burst of speed? This is using centrifugal force.

WHAT IS MARS LIKE?

Scientists have studied Mars for many years. They have sent equipment to take pictures and measurements, and to test small samples of its atmosphere and land. Scientists estimate that the gravity on Mars is about 38 percent of the gravity on Earth. That means that something that weighs 100 pounds on Earth (45 kilograms) would weigh about 38 pounds on Mars (17 kilograms).

Because there is less gravitational pull on Mars, it has bigger mountains! Mount Everest is the highest mountain on Earth. When measured from the bottom of the sea to its peak, it is 8 miles tall (over 13 kilometers). Only about 3 miles of that is above sea level (less than 5 kilometers). Olympus Mons on Mars is about 14 miles tall (around 22 kilometers).

OLYMPUS MONS
EVEREST

Test Centripetal Force

Centripetal force is an inward force that holds objects in place. Try swinging a ball in a cup to see centripetal force for yourself.

1 Use the hole punch to cut three holes around the rim of the cup. The holes should be equally spaced around the cup.

2 Cut three pieces of string. Tie each piece to one of the holes. Gather the other ends of the strings and tie them together.

3 Put a small ball in the cup. Hold the strings. Your hand is the earth and the strings are gravity. The cup holding your ball is the moon.

4 Rock the cup back and forth a few times to get up speed. Swing the cup in a circle in front of you. Does the ball fall out, even when it is upside down?

THINGS TO TRY: What happens if you spin the cup very slowly? What happens if you spin the cup super-fast? What happens if you use longer or shorter strings?

SUPPLIES

➚ hole punch

➚ small cup

➚ scissors

➚ string

➚ small ball

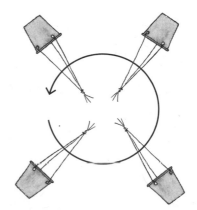

Times of Tides

It's easier for gravity to pull water than it is to pull solid things. The oceans on the earth are pulled by the gravity from the moon and sun. Since the moon is closer, its pull is twice as strong as that of the sun. When the moon and sun are lined up, the gravitational pull of the sun and moon work together. This causes the water to move more and the tide to be higher. This happens when there is a full moon and a new moon.

1 Imagine the rubber band is water. The baseball is the earth. Put the rubber band around the middle of the baseball. Make sure the rubber band is large enough that it can be pulled several inches away from the ball.

2 Tie a piece of string around the tennis ball. Cut off any extra string. The tennis ball will be the moon.

3 Tie string around the basketball. Cut off any extra string. The basketball will be the sun.

4 Cut a 6-inch piece of string (15 centimeters). Tie one end to the string around the tennis ball. Tie the other end to the rubber band around the baseball.

5 Cut a 46-inch piece of string (1 meter). Tie one end to the string around the basketball. Tie the other end directly opposite the other string tied to the rubber band on the baseball.

SUPPLIES

- ↗ wide rubber band
- ↗ baseball
- ↗ string
- ↗ tennis ball
- ↗ scissors
- ↗ basketball
- ↗ 2 friends

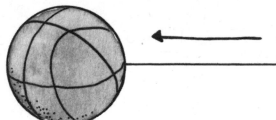

6 Have one friend hold the basketball and one friend hold the tennis ball. Stand between them and hold the baseball.

WORDS to KNOW

right angle: an angle like the corner of a square.

7 Have the friends slowly pull their balls away from you. Notice how your rubber band—which is the water—gets pulled away from the surface of the baseball. This is like gravity pulling water away from the earth and toward the sun or moon. This would be high tide.

THINGS TO TRY: Sometimes, the sun and moon are lined up on the same side of the earth. What happens to the tide when they are pulling in the same direction? Other times the sun and moon are at **right angles**, and the sun, moon, and earth make an L-shape in the sky. What happens to the tide then?

Did You Know?

Something with a weight of 100 pounds on the earth (45 kilograms) will weigh about 16 pounds on the moon (7 kilograms). This means the pull of gravity on the moon is one-sixth as strong as the pull of gravity on the earth. Neil Armstrong's 180-pound suit (82 kilograms) felt like only 29 pounds on the moon (13 kilograms).

ACTIVITY

Mock Earth Orbit

Now that you know how things orbit, create a model and see how well you can control the forces at work!

1 Trace the bottom of the bowl on the paper.

2 Draw a picture of the earth on the circle. Cut it out.

3 Tape it to the bottom of the bowl on the inside.

4 The sides of the bowl represent space near the earth. The marble is a shuttle you want to orbit the earth. Put the marble in the bowl.

5 Start moving the bowl in a circle. The marble will start climbing the sides as it spins.

THINGS TO TRY: What happens when you spin the bowl faster? Slower? Can you turn the bowl sideways and keep it in? Can you turn it upside down? Try it again with other balls. If the ball travels too fast, it overcomes the centripetal force. It leaves the near-earth orbit of the bowl and goes sailing into space.

The force moving it away is called centrifugal force. The same thing could happen with space shuttles. If they go too fast, they could leave the earth's orbit!

SUPPLIES

↗ large bowl

↗ paper

↗ crayons

↗ scissors

↗ tape

↗ marble

Floating or Falling?

When something is in free fall, it is falling at the speed of gravity. It acts like it has no weight. It looks like it is floating in air.

Caution: This activity is messy, so you may want to do it outside.

1 Punch two holes near the bottom of the cup.

2 Fill the cup with water. What happens to the water?

3 Hold your fingers over the holes. Refill the cup.

4 Remove your fingers at the same time you drop the cup. Watch carefully as the cup falls. Does any water comes out?

SUPPLIES

↗ hole punch

↗ paper cup

↗ water

WHAT'S HAPPENING? The water and the cup are in free fall. The water is travelling at the same speed as the cup. When does the water come out?

JUST for FUN

What season is the cheapest?
Free fall.

PUTTING GRAVITY TO WORK

WORDS to KNOW

water wheel: a wheel with paddles attached that spins when water flows over it. The energy can be used to lift water, power machines, or create electricity.

trebuchet: a machine that uses weight and gravity to hurl large stones at enemies.

Even before people knew how or why gravity worked, they used it to make their lives easier. They used it to move water where they wanted it. They used falling water to power **water wheels**. They used it to fire weapons called **trebuchets**. Gravity was even put to use in cooking.

We still use gravity today in many of the same ways. Turn on a water tap. Gravity is probably helping to bring water to your sink. Turn on a light. Gravity may be helping to make the electricity the light uses. Push a window up to open it. It may not seem possible, but gravity is keeping it from falling down again.

To put gravity to work, you will use things you learned earlier in this book. Gravity is a force that is pulling you down. If you know how to use it, gravity won't hold you down for long!

Imagine that where you live, you do not have a faucet in your house or even a place to get water in your town. If you want a drink of water you have to go to the water. You might lean down and take a sip from a river or lake. With pots and water bags, you can carry water home, but you still have to go to where the water is. A long time ago people wondered, "How can we get water to come to us?" Gravity was a huge part of the answer.

If there is a lot of water up high in the mountains, you can use gravity to move the water downhill to where you want it. That's exactly what many ancient **civilizations** did. They started by simply digging ditches and tunnels to lead the water to farms and people. But what if people wanted to move the water across a valley? Gravity would pull the water down the hill on one side, but how would it get up the hill on the other side?

WORDS to KNOW

civilization: a community of people that is advanced in art, science, and government.

aqueduct: a pipeline or bridge that moves water using gravity.

People built special bridges with a channel carved into the top to move water from one side of a valley to the other. These **aqueducts** moved millions of gallons of water every year. Aqueducts are still used today, but most of them are underground pipes.

Did You Know?

The ancient Romans built some of the world's most famous aqueducts. They built hundreds of miles of aqueducts to bring clean water to Roman cities for drinking, cooking, and cleaning. The tallest bridge aqueduct was over 200 feet tall (61 meters). The longest pipeline aqueduct was almost 60 miles long (96 kilometers). You can still see many ancient stone arch aqueducts today!

TRY IT: FINDING DOWNHILL

Cut a paper cup down opposite sides and across the bottom. Cut off the bottom of each piece so that you have two curved pieces. Tape the two pieces together to make a channel. Go outside and lay them down. Pour a bit of water into the middle. Watch to see if the water moves to one end or the other. If it does, you know which way is downhill. If the water doesn't move, you can put a small rock under one end to lift it up.

WATER POWER

An aqueduct is only one way people have used gravity and water. Have you ever been near a waterfall or a dam? Then you know that moving water has a lot of power. A water wheel can use that power. Each wheel has many blades sticking out from the center. As water hits each blade, it makes the wheel spin.

At first people just hooked the spinning wheel up to saws, grinding stones, and other things that needed power to move. Today, water pouring out of the giant Hoover Dam on the border between Arizona and Nevada turns water wheels that make electricity. There are many other dams like this around the country and around the world.

GOOD-TASTING GRAVITY

Do you like turkey with gravy? One of the main parts of gravy is meat broth. Broth is mostly water, but there is some animal fat in it too. A little bit of fat in the broth adds flavor to the gravy. Too much fat makes gravy taste greasy. To get most of the fat out of the broth, cooks put gravity to work. They pour all the broth into a tall cup or jar and let it sit. Gravity pulls the water down because it's heavier. The grease floats to the top because it's lighter. All the cook has left to do is skim the grease off the top.

Did You Know?

If you put fresh whole milk in a tall jar, cream will rise to the top. You can take the cream off to make butter or whipped cream, and drink the milk!

COUNTERWEIGHTS

Have you ever been on a seesaw opposite someone much heavier than you? If you don't hang on, when they go down you can find yourself flying off! Keep this idea in mind as you learn how gravity is used to fire a weapon called a **counterweight** trebuchet.

WORDS to KNOW

counterweight: a weight that balances another weight.

Long before tanks and guns were invented, armies at war used trebuchets to shoot rocks and other things over walls and into enemy camps.

66

A trebuchet had a wooden frame that looked like the letter A. On top of the frame there was a long pole. A very heavy weight hung from one end of the pole. Soldiers pulled down the end of the pole opposite the weight and held it down. They attached a long sling with a heavy rock in a pouch. Then the pouch was placed under the middle of the A-frame. To fire the trebuchet, the soldiers let go of the lower end. Gravity quickly pulled down the heavier end. The pouch shot out from under the frame so fast that the rock stayed inside until the pole stopped moving. Then centrifugal force sent the rock sailing off, bombing the enemy town or camp.

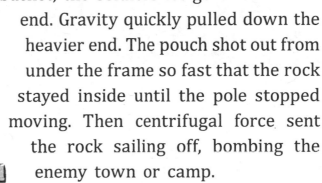

TRY IT: MARSHMALLOW TREBUCHET

Place a pencil flat on a table. Put a stiff ruler over the center of the pencil so that it looks like a seesaw. Place something very light, like a marshmallow, on one end of the ruler. Quickly push your hand down on the opposite end. What happens?

ACTIVITY

Counterweight

Some houses have windows that you push up to open. Why doesn't gravity pull the window down as soon as you let go? There might be a counterweight hidden on the side. Many counterweights work with a **pulley**.

WORDS to KNOW

pulley: a wheel with a grooved rim that holds a rope.

SUPPLIES

- ↗ pencil
- ↗ empty spool
- ↗ string
- ↗ 2 binder clips
- ↗ 2 paper cups
- ↗ 10 marbles

1 Poke the pencil through the middle of the spool. This will be your handle.

2 Tie a binder clip to each end of the string.

3 Find the middle of the string and wrap the string here one time around the spool. Try to leave even lengths of string on each side of the spool.

4 Attach one cup to each binder clip. Put three marbles in one cup and six marbles in the other cup. Lift the spool and cups off the table using the pencil handle. What happens to each cup?

5 Add one marble to a cup, pull it down, and let go. Does the other cup stay up or fall back down? Do you need to have the same number in each cup for the spool to be balanced?

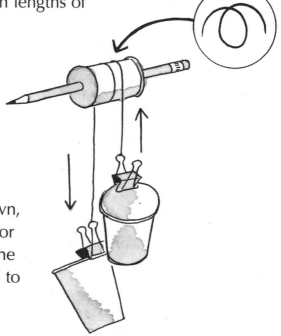

THINGS TO TRY: Can you find anywhere else counterweights are used? Here are some places to look for them. Can you think of more?

- On the scale at a doctor's office.
- Inside a grandfather clock.
- Holding the bar of lights up over a stage.
- On a construction crane.
- In an elevator shaft.

SIMPLE MACHINES

The pulley in this counterweight activity is a simple machine. A simple machine is called simple because it has very few parts. Other simple machines are the wedge, lever, screw, wheel and axle, and inclined plane. None of these machines can do anything by itself. A simple machine needs you to add your energy to make it do its job. A pulley will not lift or lower the window if you don't push up or down. But it will make it easier for the window to move and hold it in place after you let go. The inclined plane is another simple machine that helps you beat gravity. Inclined planes include ramps and slides. It takes less work to push something up an inclined plane that to lift it up, especially if you have to go a long distance.

Make a Water Tower

Instead of using aqueducts to move water, some cities store water in tall towers. They build the towers on the highest place around. They use pumps to fill the top of the tower with water. When you turn on a water tap, gravity pulls water down through pipes and to the tap. This uses less energy than having a pump pushing water through miles of pipes. Follow the steps below to make your own water tower.

SUPPLIES

↗ scissors
↗ 2 liter plastic bottle
↗ bendable straw
↗ clay
↗ water

Caution: This activity is messy so be sure to test it outside or over a sink.

1 Cut off the bottom of the plastic bottle. Hold the bottle upside down.

2 Put the short part of the straw up into the neck of the bottle. Push clay around it so that no water will leak out. Make sure that you don't block the opening of the straw with any clay.

3 Bend the straw so the long free end outside the bottle is pointing up as high as possible. Cover the end of the straw with a finger. Fill the bottle with water.

4 Lower the free end of the straw. When does the water shoot the farthest? When does it run the slowest? Does it ever stop when there is still water in the bottle?

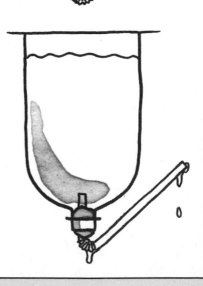

THINGS TO TRY: Most water towers serve more than one pipe. Measure the farthest distance the water can shoot with just one straw pipe. Then add a second straw to the bottleneck. How far can the water shoot with both straws open? Predict how far the water would shoot if you added a third straw pipe. Then try it!

GRAVITY WELLS

Some people get their water from **artesian wells**. These wells are like natural water towers. Water soaks into the soil on top of a hill.

It seeps straight down through the soil until it hits a layer of rock. The layer of rock acts like a slide, moving the water down the hill. The water flows downhill underground between layers of rock that don't let it escape. When

WORDS to **KNOW**

artesian well: a well drilled through rock. The water is under pressure because it is flowing downhill from higher ground.

someone near the bottom of the hill makes a hole in the rock layer above the water, water comes out of the hole. No pump is needed. Gravity did all the work.

Cantilever

Most benches that you sit on have legs right under you. A picnic table with attached benches is different. The benches don't have anything right under them. They have a **beam** that goes to the table. This is a **cantilever**.

How much mass can a cantilever support? Get ready to use what you know about gravity and center of balance to find out! Use a chart like this one to record your data.

1 The ruler is your cantilever. Lay it on a table. Move one end over the edge until it is just in balance.

2 Place four pennies on the part of the ruler that is on the table, 3 inches from the table's edge (7½ centimeters). These pennies are the support for your cantilever.

3 How many pennies do you think you can place on the unsupported part of the ruler? Try it and see. Start with one penny 3 inches from the edge of the table (7½ centimeters). Add one penny to the stack at a time. When does it tip over? In the chart, record the number of pennies in the stack before it falls (row 1, column 3).

SUPPLIES

➚ science journal and pencil

➚ flat stiff ruler

➚ table

➚ 30 pennies

WORDS to KNOW

beam: a strong piece of wood laid across posts for support.

cantilever: a beam with one end supported and the other end free.

4 Set up the ruler again. This time place four support pennies (on the table side) 2 inches from the edge (5 centimeters). Repeat the experiment by stacking one penny at a time 2 inches off the edge of the table (5 centimeters). Record your results the chart (row 2, column 3).

5 Set up the ruler one more time with four support pennies 4 inches from the edge (10 centimeters) and stack pennies 4 inches off the edge. Record your results in the chart (row 3, column 3).

6 Complete column 4 by multiplying column 2 x column 3. Compare column 4 to the number in column 1. What do you notice?

THINGS TO TRY: Try different distances and numbers of pennies. Make stacks of pennies in many places at the same time and record your results in the chart. What do you notice? Can a cantilever ever fall? Can you find a balance point where you can put no pennies on the table side and one penny on the free side without having it fall?

SUPPORTED (ON TABLE)	UNSUPPORTED (OFF TABLE)		
DISTANCE (D1) x NUMBER OF PENNIES (N1) = ?	DISTANCE (D2)	NUMBER OF PENNIES (N2)	D2 x N2 = ?
3 inches x 4 pennies = 12	3 inches		
2 inches x 4 pennies = 8	2 inches		
4 inches x 4 pennies = 16	4 inches		

Liquid Gravity

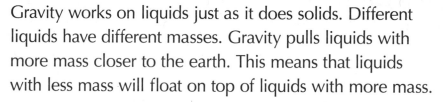

Gravity works on liquids just as it does solids. Different liquids have different masses. Gravity pulls liquids with more mass closer to the earth. This means that liquids with less mass will float on top of liquids with more mass.

1 Copy the chart shown here into your science journal to record your results.

2 Use the marker to label the cups A, B, C, and D.

3 Pour ¾ cup of water into cup A. Add a few drops of food coloring and stir with the spoon.

4 Pour ¼ cup of the colored water into cups B and C. You should have 3 plastic cups with colored water and one empty cup (D).

SUPPLIES

↗ science journal and pencil

↗ marker

↗ 4 clear plastic cups

↗ measuring cup

↗ water

↗ food coloring

↗ spoon

↗ cooking oil

↗ dark syrup

↗ baby oil

↗ clear plastic bottle

5 Pour ¼ cup of cooking oil into cup A. Let it sit for one minute. Record your observations on the chart in your journal.

6 Pour ¼ cup of syrup into cup B. Let it sit for one minute. Record your observations.

7 Pour ¼ cup of baby oil into cup C. Let it sit for one minute. Record your observations.

8 Pour ¼ cup of cooking oil and ¼ cup of baby oil into cup D. Let it sit for one minute. Record your observations.

9 Use your record chart to make predictions. When all four liquids are poured into one bottle, which one will be on the bottom? Which one will float on top? Draw your predictions, then test them by pouring ¼ cup of each liquid into the bottle. Were your predictions correct?

THINGS TO TRY: What happens if you put an ice cube in the liquid sandwich? Will the layers re-form if you shake the bottle? Do all liquids fall at the same speed? How can you use a dropper to find out?

TEST CUP	LIQUIDS TESTED	RESULTS Which is on top?
A	water and cooking oil	
B	water and syrup	
C	water and baby oil	
D	baby oil and cooking oil	
BOTTLE	water, cooking oil, syrup, and baby oil	

GREAT GRAVITY TRICKS

Now you know that any object that has mass is pulling other objects with mass closer to it. The more massive thing creates the bigger pull. That pull is called gravity. You also know you have to use some other force to get past the pull of gravity. Gravity keeps your feet on the ground, unless you use the force of your muscles to push off the ground. But you won't stay off the ground for long before gravity pulls you back down.

How can you increase your force? Jumping on a trampoline is one way. You jump higher and stay in the air longer. But the earth's gravitational pull keeps bringing you back down.

You might be thinking, wouldn't it be great if we could turn gravity off? Or invent an anti-gravity machine? But scientists agree that a world without any gravity at all would be horrible. Everything would float away unless it was tied down. The water in oceans, lakes, and rivers would float away. Even the earth's atmosphere would float away. All the air would head out into space, leaving us nothing to breathe! Sounds like the moon, right?

That doesn't keep some scientists from trying to invent an anti-gravity machine. They would like to turn off gravity for one or two things at a time. Without gravity, builders wouldn't need huge cranes to lift heavy materials. Rockets wouldn't need so much fuel to get into outer space.

If you watch movies about space, it may seem like someone has already invented an anti-gravity machine! You see people on spaceships floating in the air. Or they jump super high and have to grab onto something before they float away.

These scenes are just special effects. Filmmakers sometimes film parts of these movies on the Vomit Comet, the Zero-G airplane. Or they attach clear wires to people and things and lift them up so it looks like they're floating. They put items on clear glass plates and hold cameras in different ways to fool your mind!

No matter what they show in movies, there is no such thing as anti-gravity! You can push against gravity, pull with gravity, or even use gravity to play tricks, but you can't make it go away. In fact, there isn't anywhere in the world we can go that isn't affected by gravity. Even the moon has a weak gravitational pull.

Instead of wishing for the impossible, use what you know to challenge your family and friends! Set up a Great Gravity Game Show with some of the fun activities. Be ready to entertain and educate as you show everyone the ups and downs of gravity!

TRY IT: SPECIAL EFFECTS

Make your own special effect using a digital camera. Tape a piece of colored poster board on a wall. Hold the camera sideways and take a picture of someone pouring juice into a glass in front of the poster board. Try not to get the glass in the picture. When you show others the picture, turn it so it looks like the juice is going sideways by itself!

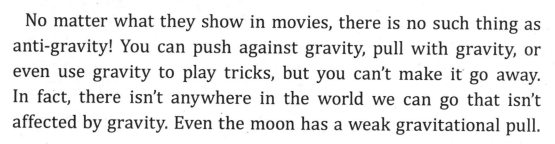

How to Spin a Basketball

You've learned about centripetal and centrifugal force. See these forces in action as you learn a fun sports skill!

1 Bend your arm at the elbow. Hold the basketball on the tips of all your fingers.

2 Twist your wrist and at the same time, push the basketball up in the air a few inches. The motion should make the basketball spin.

3 The ball should land right back in your hand if you are not throwing it too hard. Practice this twist and toss motion a few times.

4 Now as you twist and toss, point your index finger up. Quickly move this finger under the center of the ball. You want the basketball to gently land on this finger. You might need to do this many times before you get it right.

5 Once the ball is spinning on your finger, slap the side of it a few times with your other hand to keep it going. Be careful not to slap it too hard. If you do, it will go flying off into space. That is centrifugal motion at work!

ACTIVITY

Set the Bottle

Some carnival games use gravity to make it harder to win. Practice before you go and you might come home a winner! This game seems easy enough. All you have to do is pull a bottle that is lying on its side to a stand. You can't see through the bottles at the fair. Make your own see-through bottles and test their tricks.

1 Fill each bottle about ¼ full with water. Place one in the freezer on its side, one upside down and one upright. Let them freeze overnight.

2 Cut a piece of string about 18 inches long (46 centimeters). Tie one end to one end of the stick. Tie the other end to the curtain ring.

3 When the water in the bottles is frozen, take them outside. Use the chalk to draw a circle on the sidewalk that is about 1 inch bigger than the bottom of the bottle (2½ centimeters).

4 Lay one bottle on its side with its bottom edge in the middle of the circle. Put the ring over the neck of the bottle.

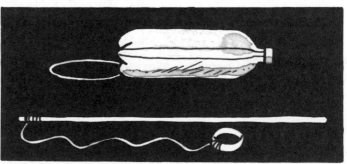

SUPPLIES

↗ 3 clear plastic drink bottles

↗ water

↗ scissors

↗ string

↗ stick

↗ shower curtain ring that fits around the necks of the bottles

↗ chalk

↗ sidewalk

↗ science journal and pencil

5 Copy the chart on the next page into your science journal and predict which bottle will be the easiest to stand up.

6 Pulling on the stick, try to lift the bottle to an upright position in the circle. Do the same thing with each bottle.

WHAT'S HAPPENING? The bottle that has ice on the top has a high center of gravity. The one with ice on the bottom has a low center of gravity. The one with ice along the side has a center of gravity somewhere along that side. Which bottle was the easiest to get standing? Which type do you think they use in the game to make it harder to win?

BOTTLE	PREDICTION	RESULT
Frozen on the side		
Frozen upside down		
Frozen upright		

Gravity Going Up?

There is an anti-gravity game called Shoot the Moon. To play the game, you try to get a marble to roll up a track made of two rods. The higher the marble climbs, the more points you get. Make your own Shoot the Moon game using funnels instead of a marble to see how it works.

1 Tape the wide mouths of the two funnels together.

2 Place the ends of the two dowel rods close to each other, but not touching. Wrap a loop of tape around these ends. There needs to be a space between the dowels that can get a little bit wider when you want it to.

3 Put a 1-inch-thick book (2½ centimeters) at one end of a table. Put the taped end of the dowel rods on this book.

4 Make a stack of books about 3 inches high (7½ centimeters) at the other end of the table. Rest the other end of the dowel rods on top of this stack.

5 Place the wide part of the taped funnels between the dowel rods on the single book.

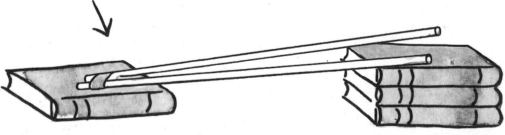

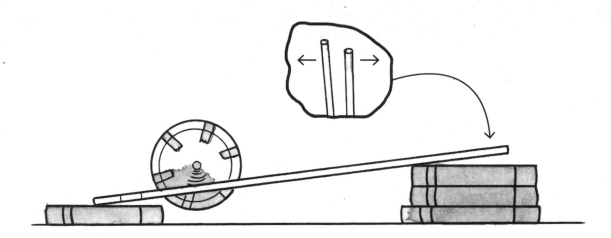

6 Slowly open the gap by moving the top ends of the dowel rods apart. Watch what happens to the funnels.

7 How far up can you get the funnels to move? What can you change to make the funnels move farther up?

WHAT'S HAPPENING? Although the funnels seem to be going against gravity, they really aren't. Try to balance the taped funnels on your two index fingers held together. Where is the center of gravity for the taped funnels? It is at the widest part.

When you put the taped funnels at the lower end of the rods, their center of gravity is on top of the rods. When you move the rods apart, gravity pulls the center of the funnels down between the rods. This makes the funnel tips go uphill while the middle part moves closer to the ground. Gravity is still working the way it always does.

THINGS TO TRY: What happens if you change the angle? How can you do this? At what point will the funnel not move up at all?

Explore Gravity Mad Lib

Fill in the blanks using as many glossary words as you can. You will end up with a silly story that may make you fall down laughing! It won't be gravity's fault this time!

noun: a person, place, or thing
plural noun: more than one noun
adjective: a word that modifies a noun (a <u>red</u> balloon)
verb: an action word
adverb: a word that modifies a verb (I walked <u>slowly</u>)

DOWN TO EARTH _____
YOUR NAME

It was a _____ day on _____. _____ was _____
     ADJECTIVE   PLACE   YOUR NAME   VERB

through the _____. All of a sudden, a _____ _____ and
        NOUN   NOUN   PAST-TENSE VERB

disappeared into _____. That's _____, thought _____.
        PLACE   ADJECTIVE   YOUR NAME

I wonder if _____ has been _____ the gravity controls again.
      PERSON ONE   -ING VERB

_____ _____ to the _____ and _____ for _____
YOUR NAME   VERB   NOUN   VERB   PERSON TWO

to come _____. _____ are _____! If you don't _____,
       ADVERB   PLURAL NOUN   ADJECTIVE   VERB

they will _____ to _____!
      VERB   PLACE

"Can you _____?" asked _____. "I will go _____ _____.
     VERB   PERSON TWO   VERB   PERSON ONE

_____ _____ to the _____."
YOUR NAME PAST-TENSE VERB   PLACE

Once there, _____ _____ the _____. By the time the
     YOUR NAME   PAST-TENSE VERB   PLURAL NOUN

_____ was done, _____ was very _____. But it was
  NOUN   YOUR NAME   ADJECTIVE

a _____ feeling to know that gravity was _____ again.
  ADJECTIVE   -ING VERB

GLOSSARY

anti-gravity: free from the force of gravity.

aqueduct: a pipeline or bridge that moves water using gravity.

artesian well: a well drilled through rock. The water is under pressure because it is flowing downhill from higher ground.

astronaut: a person who travels or works in space, where the moon, sun, planets, and stars are.

atmosphere: the blanket of air surrounding the earth.

attraction: an invisible power that pulls things together.

avalanche: a large amount of snow that slides down a mountain very quickly.

balance: a tool that shows if the mass of objects is even.

BCE: put after a date, BCE stands for Before the Common Era and counts down to zero. CE stands for Common Era and counts up from zero. The year this book was published is 2013 CE.

beam: a strong piece of wood laid across posts for support.

black hole: a place in space where gravity is so strong even light gets pulled in.

body sense: when your body sends signals to your brain to help it tell which way is up and which way is down.

calcium: a mineral found mainly in the hard part of bones.

cantilever: a beam with one end supported and the other end free.

center of balance: the point on an object where its mass is even all the way around.

center of gravity: the point on an object where it can be supported and stay in balance.

centrifugal force: the outward force on an object moving in a curved path around another object.

centripetal force: the inward force that keeps an object moving at a steady speed in a circular path around another object.

civilization: a community of people that is advanced in art, science, and government.

counterweight: a weight that balances another weight.

data: a collection of facts.

down: toward the ground. If you're underground, down means toward the center of the earth.

GLOSSARY

eardrum: the part of the ear that separates the inside of the ear from the outside.

estimate: a best guess using facts you know.

force: a push or a pull.

free fall: to be pulled through the air by only the force of gravity.

G-force: a measure of the force of gravity.

gravitational pull: the force of gravity acting on an object.

gravity: a natural force that pulls objects to the earth.

helium: a light gas often used to fill balloons.

hypothesis: a prediction or unproven idea that tries to explain certain facts or observations.

International Space Station (ISS): a science lab in orbit about 200 miles above the earth.

invisible: unable to be seen.

level: straight across, not tilted.

light year: the distance light travels in one year.

mass: the amount of matter in an object.

matter: something real that takes up space.

microgravity: when something acts like there is no gravity because it is in free fall or in orbit around the earth.

mobile: a construction or sculpture made of balanced wire and shapes that can be set in motion by the movement of air.

NASA: National Aeronautics and Space Administration, the U.S. organization in charge of space exploration.

nerve: a bundle of thread-like structures that sends messages between different parts of the body and the brain.

new moon: when the moon is directly between the earth and the sun so it is not clearly visible or seen as just a tiny sliver.

object: something that can be seen or touched.

observation: something you discover using your senses.

orbit: the path of an object circling another object.

oxygen: a gas in the air that people and animals need to breathe to stay alive.

philosopher: a person who thinks about and questions the way things are in the world and in the universe.

GLOSSARY

predict: to say what will happen before it really happens.

pulley: a wheel with a grooved rim that holds a rope.

rate: the speed of something measured in an amount of time, such as miles per hour or feet per second.

resistance: a force slowing down another force.

right angle: an angle like the corner of a square.

scientific law: a description of something that happens in nature, but not why. Scientific laws are based on observations.

scientist: someone who studies science and asks questions about the natural world, seeking answers based on facts.

sense of balance: when your eyes, ears, and body sense all work together to help you stay upright and not fall over.

space probe: a spacecraft used to explore the solar system and transmit data back to the earth.

sprout: to start growing.

stable: not likely to change.

terminal velocity: the fastest an object will travel in free fall.

theory: an idea that tries to explain why something is the way it is.

tide: the daily rise and fall of the ocean's water level near a shore.

trebuchet: a machine that uses weight and gravity to hurl large stones at enemies.

universe: everything that exists everywhere.

vacuum: a space with nothing in it, not even air!

vertical: straight up and down.

water wheel: a wheel with paddles attached that spins when water flows over it. The energy can be used to lift water, power machines, or create electricity.

weight: a measure of the gravitational pull on an object.

BOOKS

Simple Machines Made Simple. Ralph St. Andre. Teacher Ideas Press, 1993

Toys in Space: Exploring Science with the Astronauts. Carolyn Sumners. McGraw-Hill, 1997

Zero Gravity. Gloria Skurzynski. Bradbury Press, 1994

WEB SITES

Train like an astronaut!
www.nasa.gov/audience/foreducators/trainlikeanastronaut/home/index.html

Newton's Law of Gravity for Kids
suite101.com/article/newtons-laws-for-kids-gravity-a41285

How much would you weigh on different planets?
www.exploratorium.edu/ronh/weight

Upside down room illusion
www.deceptology.com/2011/09/upside-down-room-optical-illusion.html

M.C. Escher's famous prints www.mcescher.com

Astronaut microgravity training plane www.gozerog.com

VIDEOS

See how toys act in space
www.nasa.gov/multimedia/videogallery/index.html?collection_id=77731

Felix Baumgartner breaks the world record for fastest human in free fall
www.youtube.com/watch?v=FHtvDA0W34I

Astronaut David Scott drops a hammer and a feather on the moon

www.youtube.com/watch?v=5C5_dOEyAfk

PLACES TO VISIT

Carnegie Science Center (physics of sports exhibit)
www.carnegiesciencecenter.org/exhibits/highmark-sportsworks-physics

NASA Space Museum www.visitnasa.com

88

INDEX

89